HISTORY'S WEIRDEST DEATHS

ACK!

James Proud

PORTABLE
PRESS
San Diego, California

Portable Press
An imprint of Printers Row Publishing Group
10350 Barnes Canyon Road, Suite 100, San Diego, CA 92121
www.portablepress.com • e-mail: mail@portablepress.com

Printers Row Publishing Group is a division of Readerlink Distribution Services, LLC.
Portable Press is a registered trademark of Readerlink Distribution Services, LLC.

All notations of errors or omissions should be addressed to Portable Press, Editorial Department, at the above address. Author or illustration inquiries should be addressed to Summersdale Publishers Ltd, Part of Octopus Publishing Group Limited, Carmelite House, 50 Victoria Embankment, London, EC4Y 0DZ, UK • www.summersdale.com

Publisher: Peter Norton
Associate Publisher: Ana Parker
Developmental Editor: April Farr
Production Team: Jonathan Lopes, Rusty von Dyl

Library of Congress Cataloging-in-Publication Data available on request.

ISBN: 978-1-68412-757-3

Printed in China

23 22 21 20 19   1 2 3 4 5

INTRODUCTION

In the time it takes you to read this sentence, five people will have died somewhere in the world. They probably passed away quite peacefully in thankfully boring ways, but occasionally humans shuffle off this mortal coil in a more interesting fashion. This book contains a choice selection of particularly noteworthy deaths from around the globe, spanning the ancient world to the present day. Some of these exits serve as tragic warnings from beyond the grave, such as the sword swallower who took on a violin bow, and some are unbelievable accidents, like the farmer killed by her own sheep. And some are so shocking that they don't belong in the introduction. What they all have in common is that they are very, very unusual. Enter – if you dare! – the world of the dead.

THE WIRE

MICHAEL ANDERSON GODWIN
Date of Death (D.O.D.) 5 March 1989

Godwin was serving time for murder in a South Carolina jail after narrowly escaping the electric chair on appeal. Six years into his sentence, a routine check found him dead in his cell, sitting naked on his metal toilet with a badly burned mouth. It transpired that while trying to fix a pair of earphones attached to his TV, the convict had bitten into a live wire and was killed in his own electric chair.

TRAGICOMEDY

ALEX MITCHELL
D.O.D. 24 March 1975

Alex Mitchell was watching an episode of the comedy show *The Goodies* at home in Norfolk when a particularly funny sketch involving bagpipes sent him into a fit of hysterics. His wife didn't find it funny when he laughed himself into cardiac arrest, but she later sent a letter to the show to thank them for making her husband's final moments so amusing.

DID YOU KNOW?

Legend has it that the eccentric Scottish Royalist Thomas Urquhart died from a laughing fit in 1660 after hearing that Charles II had been restored to the throne.

DID YOU KNOW?

- *You are more likely to be killed by a cow, a champagne cork, a ballpoint pen, hot tap water, a vending machine or being left-handed than by a shark.*

- *More people die in the first week of the year than any other.*

- *People are most likely to die in the morning, around 11 a.m.*

- *Monday is the most common day to suffer a fatal heart attack.*

- *If you are over 60, you are more likely to die on your birthday than any other day. Nobody is sure why, but theories include the psychological effects of reaching a milestone and the dangers of overindulgence on the big day.*

SKY DIED

REGINALD CHUA
D.O.D. 25 MAY 2000

Three hundred passengers on a flight in the Philippines were terrorized by an armed man wearing a balaclava and swimming goggles who threatened to detonate a grenade unless they gave him money. The hijacker then told the pilot to fly at a lower altitude so that he could escape with the swag, and donned what appeared to be a home-made parachute. He was reluctant to jump, so one of the crew helped him on his way with a shove. The robber's body was found embedded in mud the next day, having fallen from 5,900 feet. His makeshift canopy had failed to open.

PAIN OF THRONES

GYÖRGY DÓZSA
D.O.D. 1514

Hungarian hero Dózsa was the leader of a failed peasant uprising against the ruling classes. After his defeat he was made an example of. A red-hot crown was forced on to his head, and he was tied to an iron throne, which was heated until his body started to cook. To add insult to injury, his fellow rebels were forced to eat the charred flesh from his bones before he died.

WATER WAY
TO GO

JENNIFER STRANGE
D.O.D. 12 January 2007

Twenty-eight-year-old mother Jennifer Strange took part in a contest called "Hold Your Wee for a Wii" on a live radio show to try to win a games console for her family. The winner would be the person who drank the most water without taking a leak. After drinking almost 2.5 gallons in three hours, Strange complained of feeling ill and failed to win the contest. A few hours later, she collapsed and died of water intoxication.

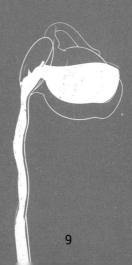

TOXIC TOADS

UNIDENTIFIED
D.O.D. MARCH 2017

A man died after eating a highly poisonous species of toad caught from a reservoir near Daejeon in South Korea. The unidentified 57-year-old had been fishing with friends for bullfrogs, an edible delicacy, which he then took to a local restaurant for preparation. Unfortunately, bullfrogs look very similar to the Korean water toad, the skin of which contains a deadly poison, and he had caught both. After eating his dish of bullfrogs, he began vomiting violently, was taken to hospital and died early the next morning.

THE HUMAN OVEN

VLADIMIR LADYZHENSKIY
D.O.D. 7 August 2010

In Finland, sitting in saunas is a competitive sport. At the 2010 world championships in Heinola, two men were left sitting in the 110°C heat: the home favorite and reigning champ Timo Kaukonen and Vladimir Ladyzhenskiy from Siberia. The Russian lasted the longest but the new champion was in no condition to celebrate, and both men passed out after suffering extensive burns. Kaukonen awoke from a coma several weeks later, but Ladyzhenskiy died as a result. It was the last ever such event.

A GAME OF
TWO HALVES

BENA TSHADI FC
D.O.D. 25 October 1998

The soccer team Basanga were hosting Bena Tshadi in a match in the Democratic Republic of Congo. The score was 1–1 when a bolt of lightning struck the pitch, knocking the players off their feet. As the Basanga players slowly recovered, they realized that the entire away team had been killed, while they had survived unscathed. Local media speculated that witchcraft was to blame.

DID YOU KNOW?

- *Cotard's Delusion, or "walking corpse syndrome," is a mental condition in which the patient believes they are dead.*

- *Botulinum Neurotoxin type H, similar to that used in Botox treatments, is so toxic that just 4 pounds of it would be enough to kill every person on earth.*

- *Eighteen people died playing American football at US colleges during 1905.*

- *A storm of giant hailstones killed 246 people (plus 1,600 cattle and sheep) in Moradabad, India, in 1888.*

- *Devastating tornadoes caused four deaths in North Texas in March 2000. Juan Carlos Oseguera from Honduras ran for cover when the storm hit, but he was struck on the head by a hailstone the size of a baseball and died the next day.*

SUGARY GRAVE

NATASHA HARRIS
D.O.D. FEBRUARY 2010

A coroner in New Zealand found that a habit of drinking up to 2.6 gallons of Coca-Cola a day was a "substantial factor" in the premature death of Natasha Harris, who suffered a cardiac arrest at the age of 30. The coroner revealed that Harris would suffer withdrawal symptoms if she ran out of the drink, and that her teeth had fallen out as a result of her addiction. The amounts of caffeine and sugar Harris was reported to have been drinking daily were equivalent to downing ten cups of coffee and a whole bag of sugar.

OWW DE TOILETTE

EDMUND IRONSIDE
D.O.D. 30 November 1016

In the eleventh century, the young King Edmund II ruled southern England in a fragile truce with the Viking King Canute. At least, he did for a few months – until he became one of history's most undignified murder victims. A traitorous nobleman called Eadric told his son to crawl into the cesspit underneath a privy (a medieval toilet) and wait for the king to do his business. When unsuspecting Edmund dropped his trousers, the youth stuck a sword into his bowels from below.

GOING UNDERGROUND

DANIEL JONES
D.O.D. 7 August 1997

One minute, you're happily digging a hole at the beach; the next, you've buried yourself alive. Daniel Jones was sitting at the bottom of the 8-feet-deep hole he had dug in the beach at Buxton, North Carolina, when his sandy excavations collapsed on top of him. Fellow beachgoers frantically tried to reach him, but to no avail. It took rescue workers with heavy equipment an hour to finally dig him out, but he had suffocated already.

I REST
MY CASE

CLEMENT VALLANDIGHAM
D.O.D. 17 June 1871

Clement Vallandigham was a distinguished Ohio lawyer whose dedication to the job would be the end of him. In 1871 he defended a man accused of shooting someone dead during a card game, and he went to great lengths to get his man off the charge. Vallandigham suspected that the victim shot himself in the stomach when drawing his own weapon, and he conducted his own experiments to prove it. He demonstrated his theory to colleagues by drawing a gun from his own pocket, as the victim might have done, and pulling the trigger. Unfortunately, the gun was loaded and he shot himself in the stomach. Vallandigham's demonstration won the case, but he died the next day from his injuries.

SHOCK 'N' ROLL

LESLIE HARVEY
D.O.D. 3 May 1972

The Stone the Crows guitarist was playing a gig in Swansea when he touched an ungrounded microphone and was electrocuted. A roadie unplugged his guitar to try to save him, but it was too late and he collapsed onstage, dying later in hospital.

BULLETPROOF

ALEOBIGA ABERIMA
D.O.D. MARCH 2001

Aberima asked a local witch doctor in his native Ghana if he could cast a spell that would render him impervious to bullets. The witch doctor set to work – presumably safe in the knowledge that the spell would never be put to the test – and smeared an herbal lotion on the patient's skin over several days. Unfortunately for both of them, Aberima asked a friend to shoot him to test the spell. Surprisingly, it didn't work, and the doctor was almost beaten to death himself by angry villagers.

VEGGING OUT

BASIL BROWN
D.O.D. February 1974

Scientific adviser Basil Brown, from Surrey, was fanatical about his health. He began drinking a lot of carrot juice because he thought he was deficient in vitamin A – up to 4.5 liters of juice a day, topped up with vast amounts of vitamin pills. He drank so much carrot juice that his body couldn't process it, causing him to turn bright yellow and die of cirrhosis of the liver. A doctor had warned him that his liver was becoming enlarged, but, as the inquest was told, "he had a low opinion of doctors."

UNUSUAL CUSTOMS

- *The Yanomami people of the Amazon drink the cremated ashes of their dead with banana juice at funeral ceremonies.*

- *The Änga people of Papua New Guinea traditionally mummified their dead relatives by smoking them over a fire. They wore their fingers as jewellery.*

- *The Malagasy people of Madagascar exhume their dead every few years. The bodies are wrapped in fresh cloth, sprayed with perfume and wine, and then relatives dance with the bones of their ancestors.*

- *In Indonesia, the Batak people ritually dig up the bodies of their dead relatives, clean their bones and move them to a new burial site.*

- *The native people of the Philippines have many different funeral traditions. In Benguet province, dead bodies are blindfolded then propped up in a chair outside their house for a week before the funeral. The Ilongot people are buried sitting up. The Isneg people of Apayao bury their dead underneath their kitchens; while in the mountains of Sagada, the dead are put to rest in coffins hanging from cliffs.*

KNIGHTS OUT

PAUL ALLEN
D.O.D. 20 September 2007

Paul Allen, 54, was a history enthusiast who enjoyed military re-enactments. In 2007, he took part in a medieval jousting demonstration for the *Time Team* TV show, using light balsa wood lances for safety. As he rode into his adversary's lance, it shattered on impact with his shield as required, but a splinter flew through a slit in his helmet, penetrated his eye and lodged in his brain. He was taken to hospital but died a week later. Hundreds of people wearing historical costumes attended his funeral.

SMOKING IS BAD FOR YOU

GARY ALLEN BANNING
D.O.D. 28 FEBRUARY 2012

Forty-three-year-old Banning was at a friend's house in North Carolina when he picked up a jar of gasoline from the kitchen and took a swig, mistaking the contents for a drink. He spat the fuel out in disgust, and went on with his evening. Sometime later, he decided to have a cigarette. As he lit up, he really lit up, as the gasoline residue on his clothes burst into flames. He was taken to hospital after firefighters responded to a call from a neighbor who detected the blaze, but he died the next day.

IT'S A GAS

JASON ACKERMAN AND SARA RYDMAN
D.O.D. 3 June 2006

Two students from Florida were found dead inside a giant helium balloon used to advertise an apartment complex. It appeared that Jason Ackerman and Sara Rydman had pulled the 8-foot balloon to the ground and crawled inside for a laugh. Helium gas makes your voice squeaky, but it also displaces oxygen in the bloodstream, so when the pair inhaled the amounts contained in the giant balloon, it caused them to lose consciousness and die as their brains were starved of oxygen.

KITCHEN NIGHTMARE

PHILLIP QUINN
D.O.D. 28 November 2004

Phillip Quinn, 24, of Washington, USA, was found dead in his mobile home with a shard of glass from a broken lava lamp stuck through his heart. Nobody else was present when he died, and his death was a mystery, until investigators concluded that Quinn had heated the lava lamp on a cooker. The heat had caused such pressure in the lamp that it violently exploded, sending shards of glass into Quinn's chest. The reasoning behind the risky experiment remains unknown.

PLAYING DEAD

Brandon Lee
D.O.D. 31 March 1993

Actor Brandon Lee, the son of martial arts legend Bruce, was filming a scene for *The Crow* in which his character is shot at from close range. Blank cartridges, with powder but no bullets, were required for authenticity. As the gun was "fired," Lee crumpled to the floor, fatally wounded in the stomach by a real bullet that had remained in the gun from a previous scene – the blank propelled that bullet out of the barrel and into Lee.

GIVEN A GRILLING

SAINT LAWRENCE
D.O.D. 10 August 258

Saint Lawrence was a clergyman in Rome, during the third century, who met his death after refusing to give up the treasures of his church to the authorities. The Roman prefect was so enraged by Lawrence's resistance that he had him tied to a giant gridiron and roasted over a fire. The story goes that when his torturers asked if he had suffered enough, Lawrence said, "Turn me over. I'm well done!" Suitably, he is the patron saint of chefs and comedians to this day.

RISQUÉ BUSINESS

PAUL COWLEY AND KIM FONTANA
D.O.D. 3 March 2002

An amorous couple were on a night out in Sheffield when their urges got the better of them, and they decided to get down to it in the middle of a public road. A passing off-duty paramedic stopped to tell them of the danger they were in, but they went on with their courting – until an approaching bus driver mistook the pair for "a bag of rubbish" in the dim light. The bus failed to take avoiding action, and they were both killed instantly.

HUNGRY HOGS

TERRY GARNER
D.O.D. 26 September 2012

Terry Garner was an Oregon pig farmer who owned some gigantic specimens weighing as much as 700 pounds. On the day he died, he went to feed the animals as usual, and never came back. When a relative went to the pigpen to look for Garner, what he found chilled his blood. Strewn amongst the snuffling sows were Garner's personal items, a pair of dentures and what remained of the man himself – which wasn't much. Not even enough, in fact, to determine a cause of death. All we know is that the 69-year-old farmer was eaten by his own pigs.

FIGHTING BLIND

JOHN OF BOHEMIA
D.O.D. 26 AUGUST 1346

King John I of Bohemia had been blind for several years before he met his end at the Battle of Crécy. He was determined not to be left out of the fun, so he ordered his men to tie their horses to his own, in order that he could ride into battle with them. They all died at the hands of the English and were found still tied together the next morning.

THE EMPEROR'S NEW PILLS

QIN SHI HUANG
D.O.D. 210 BCE

Huang was the first emperor of China, the man famous for building the Great Wall and being buried with thousands of terracotta warriors. He became paranoid about death after surviving three assassination attempts, and sought out herbs and potions from far and wide in his search for a life-giving elixir. One such "cure" was mercury pills, a surprisingly common treatment at the time. It's unclear why Huang thought eating the toxic metal would be a good idea — but it wasn't, and he fatally poisoned himself.

31

DID YOU KNOW?

- In 897, Pope Stephen VI exhumed his penultimate predecessor, Formosus, and put him on trial for being a bad pope. He was found guilty.

- In 1920, 10,000 people attended the funeral of a canary called Jimmy in Newark, New Jersey.

- It is legal to marry a dead person in France – if the wedding was planned before their death.

- Before he became the president of the USA in 1885, Grover Cleveland acted as executioner as part of his duties while sheriff of Erie County, and hanged two people.

DANCE TILL YOU DROP

HOMER MOREHOUSE
D.O.D. 14 April 1923

In the 1920s, a new fad of dance marathons took hold in the USA. Couples would dance for as long as they could, with only short breaks, in order to remain the last dancers standing and claim a prize. Some competitions lasted for several weeks at a time. One of several casualties was 27-year-old Homer Morehouse of New York, who dropped down dead from heart failure upon leaving the dance floor after 87 hours of jiving.

CASKET FALL

HENRY TAYLOR
D.O.D. 19 October 1872

An extra death haunted a funeral in a London cemetery when one of the pall-bearers, 60-year-old Henry Taylor, tripped on a gravestone and fell as the coffin was transported along a narrow path towards the grave. His fellow coffin carriers lost control of the casket and dropped it on top of him. After some confusion, the burial continued as planned while Taylor was taken to hospital, but he died of his injuries a few days later.

DISAPPEARING ACT

CHARLES ROWAN
D.O.D. 1930

The South African Charles Rowan performed as Karr the Magician. One of his tricks was to escape from a straitjacket as a car accelerated towards him. His last performance was in Springfontein in front of a large crowd. He managed to wriggle free from the jacket with seconds to spare, which unfortunately wasn't enough. The car struck him and "almost severed" his right leg, and he quickly succumbed to his injuries.

MAKING A SPLASH

CHARLES STEPHENS
D.O.D. 11 July 1920

Charles Stephens, a 58-year-old English barber and amateur daredevil, went over Niagara Falls in a barrel in 1920. He optimistically wanted to remain upright, so he installed straps for his arms and tied an anvil to his feet for ballast. Stephens plunged into the pool at the bottom of the falls with such force that the anvil smashed through the bottom of the barrel and took the barber with it, leaving only his right arm to be found.

NIAGARA FAIL

GEORGE A. STATHAKIS
D.O.D. 5 July 1930

When George A. Stathakis plunged over Niagara Falls in a home-made barrel, the 46-year-old chef from New York was accompanied for unknown reasons by his pet turtle Sonny. His custom barrel was ten feet long, reinforced with steel, and said to weigh a ton. Its strength ensured that Stathakis survived the 165-foot drop, but the heavy barrel didn't emerge from the maelstrom until the next morning, by which time he had suffocated. Incredibly, Sonny is reported to have survived the fall.

ISN'T IT IRONIC

BOBBY LEACH
D.O.D. April 1926

Bobby Leach was an English stuntman who went over Niagara Falls in a barrel in July 1911. But the fall didn't kill him (though it took six months for him to recover from his injuries), and he became only the second person to survive the trip. He went on to perform other death-defying feats, including several failed attempts at swimming the Niagara rapids, and toured the world regaling audiences with the tales of his escapades. In 1926, Leach's luck ran out after slipping on a banana peel and breaking his leg in New Zealand. The injury became infected and he died two months later.

BAD AIM

KAREL SOUCEK
D.O.D. 20 JANUARY 1985

In 1984, Canadian Karel Soucek survived going over Niagara Falls in a barrel unscathed. So why is he in this book? The following year, Soucek planned a stunt where he would be nailed into another barrel and dropped from 180 feet into a water tank just 12 feet wide. As the barrel plunged towards the ground, it spun off target and bounced off the side of the tank on to the ground. The 45,000-strong crowd applauded the stunt, but realized that things had not gone to plan when paramedics rushed on to the scene and carried the daredevil away. Soucek suffered terrible crush injuries and a fractured skull, from which he did not recover.

MAD
SCIENTIST

JESSE WILLIAM LAZEAR
D.O.D. September 1900

Scientist Jesse William Lazear worked at a US Army barracks in Cuba, where he was part of a team investigating the deadly yellow fever that its troops were suffering from. He was so determined to prove his theory that mosquitoes were responsible for the illness that he deliberately allowed the bugs to bite him in order to study the disease in his own body. Sure enough, he soon contracted yellow fever, triumphantly proving his theory – but bringing about his own death within a couple of weeks.

OLIVE
TWIST

SHERWOOD ANDERSON
D.O.D. 8 March 1941

The American novelist Sherwood Anderson committed the grave error of making a meal of a cocktail on board a ship bound for South America. He swallowed a 3-inch toothpick from an olive while drinking a Martini, his favorite drink. He developed terrible stomach pains, and died in Panama of peritonitis.

DEAD LEG

Sir Arthur Aston
D.O.D. 10 September 1649

During the invasion of Ireland in the English Civil War, Oliver Cromwell's Roundhead forces laid siege to Drogheda. The town was held by Royalist troops under the command of Sir Arthur Aston, who had lost a leg earlier in the campaign and was rumored to keep gold coins in the replacement wooden limb. Cromwell offered to let Aston surrender, but the veteran refused. When the Roundheads finally breached the town walls and found Aston, they seized his wooden leg and "beat his brains out" with it.

LAVA LEAP

EMPEDOCLES
D.O.D. 430 BCE

Empedocles was a Greek philosopher from the island of Sicily. He believed that death was caused by the cooling of the blood; therefore it followed that by jumping into the active volcanic crater of Mount Etna you would become a god and live for ever. It's not certain whether Empedocles was successful, but he certainly moved on from this life in one way or another.

UNLUCKY LETTER

THAN SINGH
D.O.D. June 2010

Seventy-year-old Than Singh of India was surprised to receive a letter from a local crematorium, as none of his family or friends had died recently. When he opened it, he was shocked to see that it was a receipt for his own cremation – so shocked, in fact, that he suffered a heart attack and died later in hospital. When Singh was cremated for real, in the very same crematorium, his family received another receipt, with the same serial number.

PIPE DRAMA

RAY LANGSTON
D.O.D. September 1996

Ray Langston's day went from bad to really, really bad after he dropped his car keys down a drain outside his brother's house in Detroit, Michigan. The 41-year-old managed to hoist open the 132-pound drain cover using a coat hanger, and squeezed his body into the 18-inch-wide hole. But as he stretched for his keys, he fell down the pipe, pinning himself head first in the sewer water. Despite his brother's efforts to shift him, Ray was stuck fast, and he drowned in 2 feet of water.

THE HYPOCHONDRIAC

MOLIÈRE
D.O.D. 17 FEBRUARY 1673

The French playwright and actor Molière suffered from tuberculosis for many years, and, unsurprisingly, it caused his death. More surprising were the time and place of his demise. He collapsed in a bloody coughing fit onstage during a performance of *The Imaginary Invalid*, a new play he had written, in which he played a hypochondriac constantly suffering from "illness." Molière managed to complete the show, but died later that day.

DID YOU KNOW?

- *It's estimated that 50,000 people were burned as witches in Europe between 1450 and 1750, and 20 percent of them were men.*

- *Powder made by grinding up ancient Egyptian mummies became a popular medicine in Europe in the sixteenth century and was still in use as late as the twentieth century.*

- *In 1900, the average global life expectancy was 31 years.*

- *A small number of people still die of the Black Death every year in the USA.*

- *The last execution by guillotine in France took place in 1977.*

FEEDING TIME

NORDIN MONTONG
D.O.D. 13 November 2008

A Malaysian cleaner who worked at Singapore Zoo gave up his life in a bizarre fashion when he jumped into an enclosure containing three gigantic white tigers. The big cats immediately started to play with their new toy, who had only a bucket and broom for protection. By the time the tigers were distracted by keepers, they had inflicted fatal injuries.

PLANT POWER

DAVID GRUNDMAN
D.O.D. 1982

David Grundman and his friend James Suchochi were playing around with guns in the desert in Arizona, taking potshots at the large saguaro cacti that grow in the area, a practice known as "cactus plugging." Grundman took aim at one old specimen that stood more than 23 feet high, and blew a heavy branch off with his first shot. He was standing too close, however, and the spiky limb crushed him to death.

PAIN IN THE NECK

PATRICK MULRANEY
D.O.D. 29 June 1891

Mulraney was a circus juggler and sword swallower who set aside his swords during a performance in Columbus, Ohio, and endeavored to swallow a violin bow instead. After trying and failing twice on account of the pain, he began to cough up blood in front of the horrified audience. Mulraney continued to suffer in this fashion until the next morning, when he died.

TIGHT SPOT

JOHN JONES
D.O.D. 25 NOVEMBER 2009

John Jones was part of a group of cavers crawling through underground tunnels at a popular site in Utah. He branched off on his own and squeezed head-first through a downward-sloping passage just 18 by 9 inches. It was a dead end, but as he tried to back out, Jones realized he was stuck fast. His friends tried and failed to shift him, and despite the efforts of 50 rescue workers he remained trapped 125 feet below ground. After 28 hours, Jones lost consciousness, and his rescuers had to concede defeat. His body was never recovered, and the cave was permanently sealed.

BUNGEE BUNGLE

MICHAEL LUSH
D.O.D. 13 November 1986

In the 1980s, the BBC program *The Late, Late Breakfast Show* enlisted and trained members of the public to perform genuinely dangerous stunts live on TV. Michael Lush, a builder, was one of those chosen. He was to escape from a box suspended by a crane 118 feet above the ground before it "exploded" then jump to the ground on a bungee rope. During rehearsals, he managed to escape from the box but fell to his death when the rope came loose. The series was cancelled as a result of the tragedy.

WORK SUCKS

RAVI SUBRAMANIAN
D.O.D. 16 December 2015

The crew of Air India flight 619 from Mumbai to Hyderabad were running late due to a scheduling clash. They rushed to the cockpit and prepared for take-off. In his haste to get going, the co-pilot mistook a gesture from the ground crew for a thumbs-up all-clear signal, and started the engine while someone was still working under the plane. Technician Ravi Subramanian was sucked into the jet engine's turbine and obliterated.

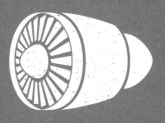

DEEP FREEZE

CHELSEA AKE-SALVACION
D.O.D. 20 October 2015

Whole-body cryotherapy involves exposing the body to extremely cold air (below −100°C) in liquid nitrogen tanks for up to 4 minutes at a time. The process is supposed to burn calories, reduce inflammation and prevent ageing. Las Vegas cryotherapist Chelsea Ake-Salvacion texted her boyfriend while working late one evening to say that she was going to use one of the pods. He never heard from her again. The next morning, colleagues found her frozen solid at the bottom of the tank. It's thought that Ake-Salvacion died from asphyxiation due to inhaling the noxious gas produced by the liquid nitrogen.

RUN THROUGH

JON DESBOROUGH
D.O.D. 10 JUNE 1999

Pupils at a Liverpool school were being shown how to throw the javelin in a PE class. The teacher, Jon Desborough, demonstrated how to safely retrieve the javelin from the field, but as he reached for a spear sticking out of the ground, he slipped on the grass and fell on to the blunt end of the shaft. It passed through his eye socket and into his skull. Desborough was able to calmly tell his pupils to walk away and get help, but he fell into a coma and died three weeks later due to complications from his injury.

THE FINAL COUNTDOWN

UNIDENTIFIED TERRORISTS
D.O.D. 5 September 1999

In 1999, a gang of Palestinian terrorists were planning twin bomb attacks on buses in two Israeli cities. One group would build the bombs in Palestinian territory, and another group was tasked with planting them on buses in Israel. What neither realized was that while the timed devices were set to Palestinian summertime, clocks in Israel – and the courier's watches – had already been switched to standard time. The bombs exploded as programmed, but an hour too early for the terrorists. They were still en route to the bus stations, and three out of the four plotters were killed.

BEWARE OF THE BIRD

PHILLIP MCCLEAN
D.O.D. 6 April 1926

The cassowary is a large flightless bird of Australasia – with a fearsome reputation. It will use its powerful legs and razor-sharp talons to kick at anything it considers a threat, including humans. In 1926 in North Queensland, 16-year-old Phillip McClean came across a cassowary in his garden and decided to attack it with a club. The bird lashed out and Phillip tripped and fell, whereupon the cassowary kicked him in the neck and severed an artery. He bled to death, becoming one of the few people ever to be killed by a bird.

FAULTY LOGIC

KURT GÖDEL
D.O.D. 14 JANUARY 1978

Austrian American Kurt Gödel was a world-famous mathematician and logical philosopher. As he grew older, he began to suffer from paranoid delusions and developed an illogical fear of being poisoned, only eating food that had been prepared by his wife, Adele. When, in his seventies, his wife was hospitalized, Gödel refused to eat anything provided by anybody else. Unfortunately, Adele was in hospital for so long that by the time she returned, Gödel weighed only 66 pounds. He was admitted to hospital, but died two weeks later of malnutrition and exhaustion.

DIE DIVE

IVAN LESTER MCGUIRE
D.O.D. 2 April 1988

He was an experienced skydiver with hundreds of jumps under his belt, but Ivan Lester McGuire made one jump too many. On the day in question, he was videoing a student, with a helmet camera and recording equipment in his backpack – this was way back in 1988. The recovered footage shows McGuire jumping from the plane, but his parachute never opens... because there was no parachute – he had forgotten to pack one. It's speculated that a combination of tiredness and confusion caused by the weight of the camera equipment in his backpack led to the fatal error.

HEAVY METAL

FREDERICK I
D.O.D. 10 June 1190

In the twelfth century, during the Third Crusade, the King of Germany and Holy Roman Emperor Frederick I led an army to recapture Jerusalem from the Muslim leader Saladin. His mighty forces swept aside all before them, until they came to the River Saleph (in present-day Turkey). As his horse waded across, Frederick I fell into the water and drowned, weighed down by his armor. His troops' participation in the Crusade ended with his death and the Third Crusade failed to capture the holy city.

TENNIS FALL

DICK WERTHEIM
D.O.D. 15 September 1983

During the boys' final at the 1983 US Open, a young Stefan Edberg of Sweden sent down a serve that struck line judge Dick Wertheim so hard in the groin that he fell from his chair and struck his head on the hard court surface. He suffered brain damage and died a week later. Edberg would go on to win the men's championships twice.

LOST
HIS HEAD

TERRY KATH
D.O.D. 23 JANUARY 1978

Terry Kath, the guitarist with rock band Chicago, was at a friend's party in Los Angeles. At the end of the evening, gun nut Kath started to play with a couple of firearms he had with him, putting an empty pistol to his head and playing Russian roulette. When he picked up a 9-mm automatic, his friend told him to be careful. "Don't worry, it's not loaded," he said, showing an empty magazine. Kath put the barrel to his head and pulled the trigger. Unfortunately, there was a bullet already in the chamber and he died instantly.

YOU SWING ME RIGHT ROUND...

WILLIAM SNYDER
D.O.D. January 1854

If you suffer from coulrophobia (an irrational fear of clowns), look away now. According to his intriguing death certificate, 13-year-old William Snyder of Cincinnati, Ohio, died in 1854 after "being swung around by the heels by a circus clown." The exact cause of death – whether he died of sheer fright, or when the clown let go mid-swing – is not recorded.

CRIMINAL DAMAGE

SANTIAGO ALVARADO
D.O.D. 3 February 1997

Twenty-five-year-old Santiago Alvarado died in the process of burgling a bike shop in Lompoc, California. It appeared that he fell as he tried to enter the shop through the roof at night. As he hit the floor, the flashlight held in his mouth was driven back into his throat with such force that it broke his neck.

ALCOHOL ABUSE

GEORGE PLANTAGENET
D.O.D. 18 February 1478

George Plantagenet, duke of Clarence, took part in more than one rebellion against his brother, King Edward IV, and was eventually convicted of treason. He was executed, but in a more imaginative – and expensive – fashion than was normal at the time. He was drowned in a barrel of malmsey wine, reportedly at his own request.

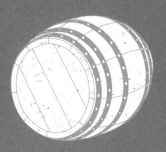

UNUSUAL METHODS OF EXECUTION

- **Crushed by elephant** *(southern Asia) – a practice that continued until the nineteenth century.*

- **The brazen bull** *(ancient Greece) – victims were cooked alive inside a bronze bull, their screams issuing from its mouth.*

- **Rat torture** *(Europe) – during the sixteenth century, hungry rats were placed on the victim's belly, under an upturned bucket upon which red-hot coals were piled (to force the rats to gnaw their way away from the heat).*

- **Death by a thousand cuts** *(China) – victims were tied up in public and sliced up slowly until they died, a custom that was finally outlawed in 1905.*

DANCE MACABRE

JEAN-BAPTISTE LULLY
D.O.D. 22 MARCH 1687

Lully was a renowned composer and ballet dancer at the court of the French King Louis XIV. He was leading a performance in a Paris church when enthusiastic conducting led him to crush his toe with the long stick he used to keep rhythm with the music. He contracted gangrene of the foot, possibly because he refused to give up dancing, and court doctors recommended amputation. The keen dancer refused treatment, and it proved to be the death of him.

FROZEN CHICKEN

FRANCIS BACON
D.O.D. 9 April 1626

The renowned Elizabethan polymath, writer and philosopher of science liked to carry out his own experiments. One winter, Bacon was traveling through a snowy London when he had an idea: why not use the cold white stuff to preserve meat? He broke from his journey, found a chicken and stuffed the carcass full of snow in an early attempt at refrigeration. Unfortunately, his chilly mission led him to contract a fatal bout of pneumonia.

UNLUCKY STARS

MARC AARONSON
D.O.D. 30 April 1987

Aaronson was a noted astronomer who observed the night sky through a giant telescope with a rotating dome in Tucson, Arizona. The revolving roof would automatically come to a stop when workers opened the door to check the weather. Aaronson died after popping outside one night just as the 500-ton dome was coasting to a halt. A ladder hanging from it smashed into the open door, which crushed him to death.

DENTAL HEALTH

AGATHOCLES
D.O.D. 289 BCE

Agathocles was an ambitious potter who became a soldier, married into wealth and then seized power by force after several attempts. The self-styled King of Sicily was a cruel ruler who was not well liked, and he met his end after using a toothpick that one of his enemies had dipped in poison. The toxin rendered him paralyzed but alive, and it was in that state that he was laid on his burning funeral pyre.

BROLLY UNLUCKY

GEORGI MARKOV
D.O.D. 11 SEPTEMBER 1978

Georgi Markov was a dissident writer from communist Bulgaria who defected to the West in the late 1960s. Ten years later, he was waiting for a bus on London's Waterloo Bridge when he felt a sharp pain in his leg. He looked around and saw a man running away with an umbrella. Later that day Markov developed a fever, and four days later he was dead. Investigations concluded that the assassin had used a modified umbrella to inject a tiny pellet containing the deadly poison ricin, for which there is no known antidote.

BEARING A GRUDGE

JÖRG JENATSCH
D.O.D. 24 January 1639

Jörg Jenatsch was a Swiss politician who made many enemies during the Thirty Years War. His deeds came back to haunt him when he attended a party during carnival season in the town of Chur. A group of men disguised in costumes entered the event, and a mysterious assassin dressed as a bear hacked Jenatsch to death with an axe.

REBEL ROBOT

ROBERT WILLIAMS
D.O.D. 25 January 1979

Robert Williams was working at a Ford Motor factory in Michigan when he was fatally struck in the head by the arm of a one-ton robot carrying car parts. Williams was hit while climbing a rack of metal castings after the machine had malfunctioned. His was the first recorded death by robot – and it would not be the last…

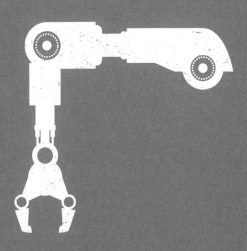

SWEET KISS OF...

FRANK HAYES
D.O.D. 4 JUNE 1923

Part-time jockey Frank Hayes was riding a 20-1-shot horse called Sweet Kiss in a steeplechase in New York state when he slumped over in the middle of the race. He had suffered a fatal heart attack but somehow remained in the saddle as Sweet Kiss jumped the remaining fences undeterred and won the race by a head. Hayes had secured his first-ever victory, but he was dead before he crossed the finish line, becoming the only known jockey to win a race after death.

EASY TIGER

HANNAH TWYNNOY
D.O.D. 23 October 1703

Hannah Twynnoy was a barmaid at the White Lion pub in Malmesbury, Wiltshire, when a traveling zoo featuring a caged tiger came to town. She was fascinated by the tiger and kept teasing it, despite being repeatedly warned of the danger. One day while she was taunting it, it escaped its enclosure and mauled her to death. Twynnoy was surely the first person to be killed by a tiger in Britain. The incident is recorded on her gravestone:

In bloom of life
She's snatch'd from hence,
She had not room
To make defence;
For Tyger fierce
Took life away,
And here she lies
In a bed of Clay,
Until the Resurrection Day.

PAIN IN THE LEG

Sigurd the Mighty, the Earl of Orkney, was killed by an enemy from beyond the grave. After defeating fellow nobleman Máel Brigte in battle, he tied his foe's decapitated head to his horse as a trophy of war. While Sigurd was riding home victorious, he grazed his leg on Brigte's teeth as he spurred his horse, inflicting a minor wound that eventually caused a fatal infection.

DID YOU KNOW?

- *When William the Conqueror died in 1087, his obese body became bloated with gas because the burial was delayed. His body burst when monks tried to fit the swollen corpse into a coffin, filling the church with a putrid stench.*

- *In 1567, Hans Steininger, the mayor of Braunau, Austria, died after tripping over his magnificent six-foot beard. He usually rolled it up to keep it out of the way, but one day a fire broke out, and in his hurry to escape he tripped over his facial hair and broke his neck. Steininger's beard is still on display in the town today.*

- *In January 1570, James Stewart, 1st Earl of Moray, was killed with a carbine (a type of early rifle) in the first successful assassination by firearm.*

- *In 1771, the renowned glutton King Adolf Frederick of Sweden died after eating a royal feast consisting of lobster, caviar, sauerkraut and herring, washed down with champagne and topped off with 14 Swedish pastries. He is thought to have died from a stroke.*

FASHION VICTIM

MARTHA MANSFIELD
D.O.D. 30 NOVEMBER 1923

Martha Mansfield, a promising young film actress, retired to a car with friends during a break in filming the American Civil War drama *The Warrens of Virginia*. Someone in the vehicle lit a match, and the heavy period dress Mansfield was wearing went up in flames. Cast and crew tried to save her, but they could not put the fire out in time and she suffered substantial burns, dying less than 24 hours later.

MONKEY BUSINESS

ALEXANDER OF GREECE
D.O.D. 25 October 1920

A healthy 27-year-old monarch, King Alexander of Greece had only reigned for three years when he was fatally injured by a pet monkey in the gardens of the royal palace in Athens. While trying to save one monkey from the jaws of his pet wolfhound, Alexander was bitten on the calf by another. The wound became infected and he contracted blood poisoning, which resulted in his death three weeks after the attack.

BALL
BOY

ALAN FISH
D.O.D. 20 May 1970

Fourteen-year-old baseball fan Alan Fish was at Dodger Stadium in Los Angeles watching the home team play the San Francisco Giants, when the Dodgers' Manny Mota hit the ball into the stands, something that normally happens a few times every game. The ball caught Fish unawares and he was struck hard on the temple, but he appeared to be OK after some aspirin and he went home with his family. Four days later he died from the injury, becoming the first and the only spectator to die after being hit by the ball at a Major League Baseball game.

DID YOU KNOW?

Ray Chapman of the Cleveland Indians is the only player to have been killed by the ball during a Major League Baseball game. In 1920, pitcher Carl Mays of the New York Yankees threw a deliberate "beanball" at Chapman's head so hard that his skull was fractured.

UDDER
TERROR

João Maria de Souza
D.O.D. 11 July 2013

João Maria de Souza was in bed with his wife in the Brazilian town of Caratinga when a cow fell through their bedroom ceiling, landing on top of him and narrowly missing his wife. The one-ton animal had wandered on to the house from the hill behind and proved too heavy for the asbestos roof. De Souza was taken to hospital with serious internal injuries and died a day later.

THE FIRST OF MANY

MARY WARD
D.O.D. 31 August 1869

The Irish astronomer Mary Ward was riding in an early steam-powered car (built by her cousins) when she was thrown from the unwieldy contraption as it navigated a corner and crushed under the wheels. The 42-year-old's untimely demise was the first recorded death from an automobile accident.

DID YOU KNOW?

Henry H. Bliss was the first person to be killed by a car in the USA. He was struck by an electric taxi in New York City in 1899.

LOOK BOTH WAYS

BRIDGET DRISCOLL
D.O.D. 17 AUGUST 1896

Bridget Driscoll, 43, became the first pedestrian to die in a motor accident in the UK when she was knocked down by a car from the Anglo-French Motor Carriage Company while crossing the road in Crystal Palace, London. The early car was traveling at no more than 5 miles per hour, because that was as fast as it could go. The coroner said that he hoped such a thing would never happen again.

DEATH FROM ABOVE

The ancient Greek Aeschylus is one of the very few people in history to have been killed by a tortoise. The celebrated Athenian playwright had heard a prophecy that he would be killed by a "falling house," and therefore spent most of his time outdoors. One day while walking under a clear sky, an eagle carrying a tortoise flew overhead. In an attempt to crack the reptile's shell, the bird dropped the tortoise on to the head of unsuspecting Aeschylus – and cracked his skull in the process.

BAD PUBLICITY

JINTARO ITOH
D.O.D. 17 September 1979

Businessman Jintaro Itoh was thinking of running for office in the Japanese general election, and he planned a risky PR stunt to gain sympathy from the public. He was to stab himself in the leg outside his home in a fake robbery then declare his candidacy as a hero from his hospital bed. When Itoh jabbed the knife into his thigh, he severed an artery and bled to death on the street.

OLD SOULS

When Thai Buddhist monk Luang Pho Daeng knew he would soon die, he decided to become a spiritual example to others. He began meditating and undertook a strict starvation diet to dry his body out, effectively mummifying himself before death. When he finally died – while meditating – he was preserved sitting in the lotus position, and he has been on display in the Wat Khunaram temple in Koh Samui ever since.

DID YOU KNOW?

The Russian writer Nikolai Gogol became increasingly eccentric in later life. The author of *Dead Souls* and *The Government Inspector* grew so delirious with obsessive prayer and religious fasting that he died of hunger in 1852 at the age of 42, having burned a manuscript he had been working on for five years.

SIX
FEET UNDER

JOE BURRUS
D.O.D. 31 OCTOBER 1990

American magician Joe Burrus planned to escape being buried alive in a tribute to Harry Houdini. He had achieved the feat a year previously, but this time he went one step further by using cement instead of soil. The event took place on Halloween at an amusement park in Fresno, California, before an excited crowd. Burrus was handcuffed, chained and placed in a transparent coffin that was lowered into a freshly dug grave. As the cement was poured in, witnesses heard a muffled crack as the plastic coffin broke under the weight, and Burrus was crushed to death.

UNUSUAL BURIALS

- *When horror film legend Bela Lugosi died in 1956, he was buried in full Dracula costume.*

- *In 1977, the Texan socialite Sandra West was buried behind the wheel of her Ferrari 330 in a San Antonio cemetery.*

- *In 1992, some of the ashes of Star Trek creator Gene Roddenberry were taken into space on a space shuttle and returned to earth. Then in 1997, a portion of his ashes was launched from a rocket to orbit around the earth.*

- *In 2008, the ashes of Fredric J. Baur of Cincinnati were buried in a Pringles tube – he had designed the packaging in the 1960s.*

- *In 2014, Billy Standley of Ohio was buried on the back of his 1967 Harley-Davidson motorcycle. His embalmed body was propped up on the seat inside a transparent coffin.*

- *The ashes of Italian tycoon Renato Bialetti, who popularized the Moka stove-top coffee maker, were interred in a giant version of his iconic coffee pot in 2016.*

HEY PRESTO?

GILBERT GENESTA
D.O.D. 9 November 1930

Gilbert Genesta was a magician from Kentucky who regularly performed the famous milk-churn escape trick. He would lower himself into a container filled to the brim with water and secured with six padlocks, leaving him 2 minutes to escape before he drowned. One night, Genesta failed to appear in time and began banging frantically to be freed. By the time helpers had forced it open, Genesta was unconscious, and he died later in hospital. The secret of the trick was a fake lid that Genesta could easily lift off, without having to undo any padlocks, when hidden from view behind a curtain. What the magician didn't know was that the milk can had been dropped by stagehands earlier in the day. The accident had damaged the fake lid, jamming it shut for real.

YOU'RE FIRED

WILLIAM ELLSWORTH ROBINSON
D.O.D. 24 MARCH 1918

The signature trick of the illusionist William Ellsworth Robinson, who performed as Chung Ling Soo, was to catch the bullets fired from two guns – with fake barrels – in his teeth. Onstage in London one night, he fell to the floor when the guns were fired, crying, "I've been shot! Lower the curtain!" He died the next day. Robinson hadn't cleaned the guns properly, and powder build-up in the fake barrels had ignited and fired real bullets.

DEAD LINE

JASON FINDLEY
D.O.D. 21 May 1985

Seventeen-year-old Jason Findley was found dead lying next to the telephone in his bedroom in New Jersey. His death was a mystery for months, until it was revealed that he had died from a lightning strike, despite the lack of visible burns on his body or damage in his room. The lightning had struck the phone line outside the house and delivered a fatal shock to his brain via the telephone receiver without leaving even a trace on the line.

PROFESSIONAL PRIDE

AMERICO SBIGOLI
D.O.D. January 1822

The Italian tenor Americo Sbigoli died during the performance of a Pacini opera. In attempting to match the first – more powerful – tenor, Sbigoli sang so hard that he burst a blood vessel in his neck and died shortly afterwards.

BIRDMAN

FRANZ REICHELT
D.O.D. 4 February 1912

Franz Reichelt of Austria believed he could fly. He designed a wing-like parachute suit and decided to test it from the Eiffel Tower in Paris. He secured permission to test his wingsuit on a dummy, but at the last moment decided to take the flight himself. After strapping the parachute to his limbs, he stepped off the edge and plummeted 187 feet to his death.

SILLY SAUSAGE

WALTER EAGLE TAIL
D.O.D. 4 JULY 2014

Forty-seven-year-old Walter Eagle Tail bit off more than he could chew when taking part in an Independence Day hot-dog-eating contest in South Dakota. In his frantic attempt to chow down more dogs than the other competitors, the speed-eating athlete stuffed too much into his mouth, choked and suffocated before paramedics could save him.

A BUG'S DEATH

EDWARD ARCHBOLD
D.O.D. 5 October 2012

A Florida reptile shop held a contest in which people competed to eat the most creepy-crawlies in order to win a python. Contestants struggled to chew through piles of cockroaches and worms, but Edward Archbold forced down the most bugs and emerged as the winner. He was unable to claim his prize, however, as he began to vomit, collapsed and died of suffocation after his airway became blocked with "arthropod body parts."

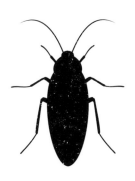

DID YOU KNOW?

- *In January 1919, a giant tank of molasses exploded in Boston, Massachusetts. The sticky tidal wave tore down buildings and killed 21 people.*

- *Hundreds of Indian children died every year after eating lychees, until in 2017 it was discovered that the popular fruit contains a toxin that is dangerous for small children to consume on an empty stomach.*

- *Several South Koreans have died while trying to eat live octopus. Problems occur when the creature's suckers stick in the throat while being swallowed.*

- *Kites annually kill several people in India – they are often garrotted by kite strings that have been coated with glass in the sport of kite-fighting.*

- *In 2009, businessman Jimi Heselden, who had made a fortune from safety barriers, bought the company that manufactures Segway scooters. A year later, he was riding one around his Yorkshire estate when he apparently lost control and rolled 39 feet over a cliff into a river. He was pronounced dead at the scene.*

DRINKY-POO

MICHAEL WARNER
D.O.D. 21 May 2004

Michael Warner of Texas died after a sherry enema. A 58-year-old alcoholic unable to swallow liquids, Warner got his wife to administer his booze from the wrong end, resulting in a blood alcohol level six times the drunk-driving limit in Texas, and fatal alcohol poisoning. According to the police, the danger of such a procedure is that the body will continue to absorb alcohol even after the person loses consciousness. Warner's wife said her husband often took alcohol in such a manner. She was accused of negligent homicide for helping Warner with the procedure, but the charges were eventually dropped.

WATCH THIS

GARRY HOY
D.O.D. 9 July 1993

Garry Hoy was a lawyer at a leading Canadian law firm, based in a 56-story skyscraper in downtown Toronto with impressive floor-to-ceiling glass windows. One evening, Hoy deployed his party trick while playing host to a group of young lawyers, shoving his body against the windows to demonstrate their strength. He took a run-up and threw his body at the glass, expecting to bounce off as usual. Unfortunately, the window gave way and the guests watched in horror as Hoy disappeared into the street below from the twenty-fourth floor.

GAME OF DEATH

Mr Hsieh
D.O.D. 8 January 2015

A certain Mr Hsieh had settled in for another long session playing online computer games at a Taiwanese internet cafe. Three days later, his fellow gamers noticed him slumped over his keyboard, but this was not unusual – they assumed he was just taking a rest. When staff finally checked on him, they discovered that he wasn't exactly resting – he was dead, and his body had already begun to stiffen. He had suffered a heart attack several hours previously but no one had noticed.

THE X-FIRES

MICHAEL FAHERTY
D.O.D. 22 December 2010

Firefighters were called to an address in Galway, Ireland, after a man reported smoke pouring from a neighbor's home. When they broke in, they discovered Michael Faherty lying dead in his living room. He had burned to death, but despite his charred remains, the only visible damage to the house was to the floor beneath him and the ceiling above. The lack of evidence meant that the authorities could find no explanation for the fatal flames, and the coroner concluded it was a case of spontaneous human combustion.

SWEET SURRENDER

MITHRIDATES
D.O.D. 401 BCE

A soldier in the Persian army who killed a prince, Mithridates was sentenced to death by scaphism – or "the boats," as it was known. He was tied up between two small boats, one on top of the other, leaving his head and limbs exposed, then force-fed milk and honey so that he would defecate or vomit, and covered in the same mixture. Then he was simply left to fester in the hot sun. Nature took its course, and after 17 days of torment he eventually died of exposure and insect infestation.

HANGING TOUGH

RAINIER HOWE
D.O.D. 4 January 1998

Twenty-year-old Rainier Howe of Melbourne, Australia, played basketball almost every night of the week, and perfected the slam dunk after years of practice. One day, he was playing with his brother and cousin when he slam-dunked the ball and hung off the ring like Michael Jordan. Unfortunately, the ring came down, along with the brick wall it was attached to, and Howe was crushed to death underneath it.

REPTILE REGRET

WAYNE ROTH

D.O.D. 8 NOVEMBER 1997

Wayne Roth was visiting a reptile collector friend who kept several large snakes in tanks when he made the serious mistake of picking up a 6-foot-long cobra, which bit him on the hand. His friend suggested he go to the hospital, but Roth told him, "I'm a man – I can handle it." They went to a bar instead, where he reportedly bragged about surviving the bite. He died later that evening from the slow-acting venom before his friend could drive him to the hospital.

DON'T FEED THE ANIMALS

XU WEIXING

D.O.D. 17 November 1999

Bus driver Xu Weixing was part of a convoy of vehicles carrying schoolchildren on a trip through a safari park in Shanghai when a tow rope came loose. Everyone knows that you are not even supposed to put your arm out of the window in a safari park, never mind get out of the vehicle, but apparently 41-year-old Weixing knew better, and he disembarked to reattach the rope in the tiger breeding area. Before he could finish the task, he was attacked by three Siberian tigers. By the time Weixing had been rescued, he was fatally injured, dying soon afterwards in hospital.

UP, UP
AND AWAY

REVEREND ADELIR ANTÔNIO DE CARLI
D.O.D. April 2008

Father Adelir Antônio de Carli was a Catholic priest from Brazil who wanted to get closer to the heavens and raise money for charity by flying 600 miles attached to 1,000 helium party balloons. Strong winds blew him helplessly off course as he soared to an altitude of 3.75 miles, and he was last heard from when he was 30 miles offshore over the Atlantic Ocean, afraid that he would crash into the sea. Rescuers found a cluster of balloons near the priest's last known position, but his body was not located for another three months.

ALL FUN AND GAMES UNTIL SOMEONE DIES

WESLEY MITCHELL
D.O.D. 10 OCTOBER 2001

A group of students at the University of the South in Tennessee were looking for some late-night high jinks, so they entered the library and decided to slide down what they assumed was a laundry chute. Wesley Mitchell was the first to jump in, and he slid all the way down... into a trash compactor that switched on automatically and crushed him to death. It was not a laundry chute.

RAMMED

BETTY STOBBS
D.O.D. 28 January 1999

Farmer Betty Stobbs of County Durham was riding a quad bike to feed her sheep in a field overlooking a disused quarry. When the hungry flock got wind of the hay bale she was transporting, they surged to the vehicle and started to push it towards the edge of the quarry. Before the farmer could escape, the flock pushed her over the cliff and the quad bike fell on top of her, killing her instantly.

THE UK'S MOST DANGEROUS JOBS

Occupation	Total deaths 2010–2016	Yearly average deaths 2010–2016
Farmer	167	27.83
Builder	101	16.83
Roofer and scaffolder	69	11.5
HGV driver	41	6.83
Carpenter and decorator	28	4.66
Mechanic	26	4.33
Electrician and plumber	26	4.33
Civil engineer	20	3.33
Trash collector	20	3.33

LEAP OF FATE

SERGEI CHALIBASHVILI
D.O.D. 16 July 1983

During the diving competition at the World University Games, the sixth-placed Soviet athlete Sergei Chalibashvili attempted an ambitious reverse 3½ somersault tuck, a dive only recently approved for competition. He leapt into the air from the 10-metre tower, but as he flipped backwards, he smacked his head on the platform and fell into the water. He never regained consciousness and died of heart failure a week later.

UNDER PRESSURE

GEORGY DOBROVOLSKY, VIKTOR
PATSAYEV AND VLADISLAV VOLKOV
D.O.D. 30 JUNE 1971

Three Soviet cosmonauts were on board the spacecraft *Soyuz 11* after time spent in the *Salyut 1* space station. They undocked from the station and told Control they were preparing to return to earth. The spacecraft completed a successful re-entry of the earth's atmosphere and landed safely, but when the hatch was opened, all three cosmonauts were dead in their seats. A valve had opened in space, causing the cabin to rapidly depressurize. They remain the only people to have died in space.

DOOMED FLIGHT

VLADIMIR KOMAROV
D.O.D. 24 April 1967

Soyuz 1 was a Soviet-manned space flight that was beset with problems from the start. The solo pilot was cosmonaut Vladimir Komarov, and the backup pilot was his friend, the legendary Yuri Gagarin. All unmanned test flights of the *Soyuz* craft had failed, and the two cosmonauts and engineers had serious reservations over the safety of a manned mission. However, political pressures meant that their concerns were ignored, and the mission went ahead as planned. According to reports, Komarov refused to back out despite his fears, because that meant sending his friend in his place. As soon as *Soyuz 1* was launched, issues with a solar panel meant that the ship did not have enough power to maneuver and could not communicate fully with earth, crippling the mission. Komarov's fate was sealed when the parachute failed on re-entry into the earth's atmosphere, leaving the craft to plummet to the ground and burst into flames, killing the cosmonaut on impact.

DEADLY ACCESSORY

ISADORA DUNCAN
D.O.D. 14 September 1927

Isadora Duncan was a flamboyant American dancer who found fame in Europe during the early twentieth century. One night, when travelling as a passenger in an open-topped car in the south of France, the long, colorful silk scarf she was wearing blew out of the cabin and became entangled in the wheels, dragging Duncan from the car and breaking her neck.

AWKWARD GUEST

JEROME I. RODALE
D.O.D. 8 June 1971

American publisher and writer Jerome I. Rodale, who advocated organic foods and healthy living, was a guest on *The Dick Cavett Show* in 1971 alongside journalist Pete Hamill. During filming, Rodale told the host that he had "decided to live to be a hundred," and that he had never felt better in his life. When he started to snore and slump in his chair, Hamill thought Rodale was joking, but he wasn't — he was dead at the age of 72. The episode, due to be aired that night, was cancelled.

DEATH METAL

KAREN WETTERHAHN
D.O.D. 8 June 1997

Karen Wetterhahn was a chemistry professor working on the effects of toxic metals. While studying the deadly compound dimethylmercury, she accidentally spilled just one or two drops of the liquid on her rubber gloves. She removed the gloves after finishing the job, but − unknown to her − the poison had already permeated the latex and been absorbed into the skin. Wetterhahn had suffered a lethal dose, but the nature of the compound meant that the poisoning took some time to take effect, and it was several months before she realized anything was wrong and linked it to the spillage. Wetterhahn was eventually admitted to hospital with acute mercury poisoning, but treatment failed, and she died ten months after exposure.

BLADE
OF GORY

VLADIMIR SMIRNOV
D.O.D. 28 JULY 1982

At the 1982 World Fencing Championships in Rome, the West German Matthias Behr was challenging the reigning champ Vladimir Smirnov of Russia. During the bout, Behr's foil snapped as he jabbed the Russian's face protector, and the jagged blade went straight through the mask, pierced Smirnov's eye socket and penetrated his brain. He was declared dead nine days later.

BLOOD SPORT

JOSÉ LUIS OCHOA
D.O.D. 30 January 2011

Cockfighting is illegal in the USA, but underground fights still take place – and it's not just the birds that are in danger. Thirty-five-year-old José Luis Ochoa suffered a fatal injury when police raided a cockfight in California in 2011. As Ochoa fled the scene, a rooster kicked him with a razor-fitted foot and sliced his leg open. Doctors were unable to stem the bleeding when he was taken to hospital, the timing of which may or may not have been delayed by the illegal nature of the activity, and he died from loss of blood.

CATA-FAULT

DINO YANKOV
D.O.D. 24 November 2002

Nineteen-year-old Dino Yankov belonged to the Oxford Stunt Factory, an unofficial dangerous sports society at Oxford University. In 2002, he volunteered along with five others to be launched from a trebuchet, a giant medieval catapult. The siege weapon used a one-ton counterweight to fling people 100 feet through the air into a large net, and had reportedly done so successfully on 50 previous occasions with only one accident. The first four people hit the net safely, but bystanders were worried that they were landing too close to the edge. When Yankov was launched, their fears were realized. He clipped the edge and fell heavily to the ground, suffering multiple injuries. He died later in hospital, and the human catapult has not been used since.

DEADLY INVENTION

VALERIAN ABAKOVSKY
D.O.D. 24 July 1921

Valerian Abakovsky was the Soviet inventor of the Aerowagon, a car-like train powered by an aircraft engine coupled to a giant propeller, capable of more than 60 miles per hour. Its maiden journey from Moscow to Tula went without a hitch, but on the return leg the contraption derailed at high speed, killing seven of the 22 passengers, including Abakovsky himself. He was given the honor of being buried in the Kremlin Wall Necropolis.

TRASH CANNED

ANASTASIO FIGUEROA
D.O.D. 14 FEBRUARY 1994

Guards at a Florida prison noticed that one of their inmates was missing soon after a trash truck had visited the facility. Lifer Anastasio Figueroa had spotted a risky opportunity to escape and jumped into the back of the truck, with predictable consequences. His crushed body was tracked down at a landfill site, and identified by his fingerprints.

BLOOD COMRADES

ALEXANDER BOGDANOV
D.O.D. 7 April 1928

Alexander Bogdanov was a Russian science-fiction writer, doctor and revolutionary, who pioneered blood transfusion during the early twentieth century. He thought sharing blood would help the workers literally bond together and extend their lives. Bogdanov gave himself several blood transfusions and claimed numerous benefits, including the prevention of baldness. When one such self-experiment used blood from a student suffering from malaria and tuberculosis, the benefits ceased.

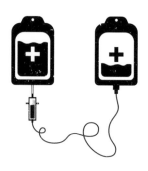

MORE UNUSUAL METHODS OF EXECUTION

- **The sack** *(ancient Rome)* – *people who had killed their parents or other close relatives were flogged and sewn into a sack with various live animals – including snakes, roosters and monkeys – then thrown into the sea.*

- **Burial** *(Europe)* – *during the Middle Ages, mothers guilty of infanticide were entombed while still alive.*

- **Hung, drawn and quartered** *(Europe)* – *in a practice used as late as the eighteenth century, criminals were dragged through the streets, hung until near death, often disemboweled, then chopped into four pieces.*

- **Death by cannon** *(India)* – *from the sixteenth century and continuing under the British empire, victims were strapped to the end of an artillery barrel and blown to pieces.*

DEADLY INGREDIENT

Peng Fan
D.O.D. August 2014

A chef at a restaurant in Guangdong, China, was preparing snake soup, the house speciality. He carefully picked the wriggling serpent out of a basket, taking care to avoid its fangs, and cut its head off. Twenty minutes later, as he threw the decapitated head away, he felt a sharp pain in his hand, and to his horror saw two puncture marks in the skin. The dead snake, a highly venomous Indochinese spitting cobra, had bitten him from beyond the grave, and he died before he could be treated. It turns out that the bite reflex of venomous snakes can be triggered hours after death, even if the head has been severed.

LAST SUPPER

BANDŌ MITSUGORŌ VIII
D.O.D. 16 January 1975

Mitsugorō was a Japanese actor, famous for his roles in kabuki theatre. He was having dinner with friends at a Kyoto restaurant when they ordered *fugu*, or pufferfish, the liver of which contains a deadly neurotoxin. Mitsugorō boasted that the poison would have no effect on him, and demanded four livers, even though the restaurant was breaking the law in serving them. He died a few hours later from the paralyzing toxin, for which there is no antidote.

DID YOU KNOW?

There were 176 deaths in Japan from eating pufferfish in 1958. There are still several cases of *fugu* poisoning every year, with ten deaths recorded between 2006 and 2015.

CHECKING OUT

MILIKA SLOAN
D.O.D. 24 June 1995

A young woman from Cincinnati, Ohio, was killed by her hotel room on her first trip away from home. Milika Sloan was returning to her room, barefooted and wet from a rainstorm, when she was electrocuted as she put her key card in the door. An inspection revealed that a faulty air-conditioning unit was discharging electricity through the concrete floor and into the door frame.

ROUGH LANDING

ROGER WALLACE
D.O.D. 18 May 2002

Roger Wallace was a radio-controlled-model-plane enthusiast whose hobby would cause his death. He was flying his 5-foot-wingspan aircraft in Tucson, Arizona, when he lost sight of it in bright sunlight as it raced towards him. Wallace saw the 6-pound plane too late to take evasive action and it struck him in the chest, causing fatal injuries.

COFFIN FIT

JOHN ORAM

D.O.D. 18 JULY 2009

When staff at a care home in Torquay heard one of their residents sneezing particularly loudly, they didn't realize it would be the end of him. But shortly afterwards, pensioner John Oram collapsed and was taken to hospital. He died two days later, and the coroner recorded that he had died from a brain aneurysm brought on by the force of a violent sneeze.

FAMOUS LAST WORDS

"I've had eighteen straight whiskies;
I think that's the record."
Dylan Thomas, poet (1953)

"They couldn't hit an elephant at this distance."
**John Sedgwick, Union Army general, just before he was shot by a
sniper during the American Civil War (1864)**

"Codeine... bourbon..."
Tallulah Bankhead, actress and hedonist – her last request (1968)

"Pardon me, sir. I did not do it on purpose."
**Marie Antoinette, queen of France, when she stepped on the
executioner's foot as she walked to her death at the guillotine
(1793)**

"I've never felt better."
Douglas Fairbanks, actor, after suffering a heart attack (1939)

"Go on, get out! Last words are for fools who
haven't said enough!"
**Karl Marx, revolutionary and philosopher, upon being asked by his
housekeeper for any last words (1883)**

"Tape *Seinfeld* for me."
Harvey Korman, actor (2008)

If you're interested in finding out
more about our books, find us on Facebook
at **Portable Press** and follow us
on Twitter at **@PortablePress**.

www.portablepress.com

Image credits